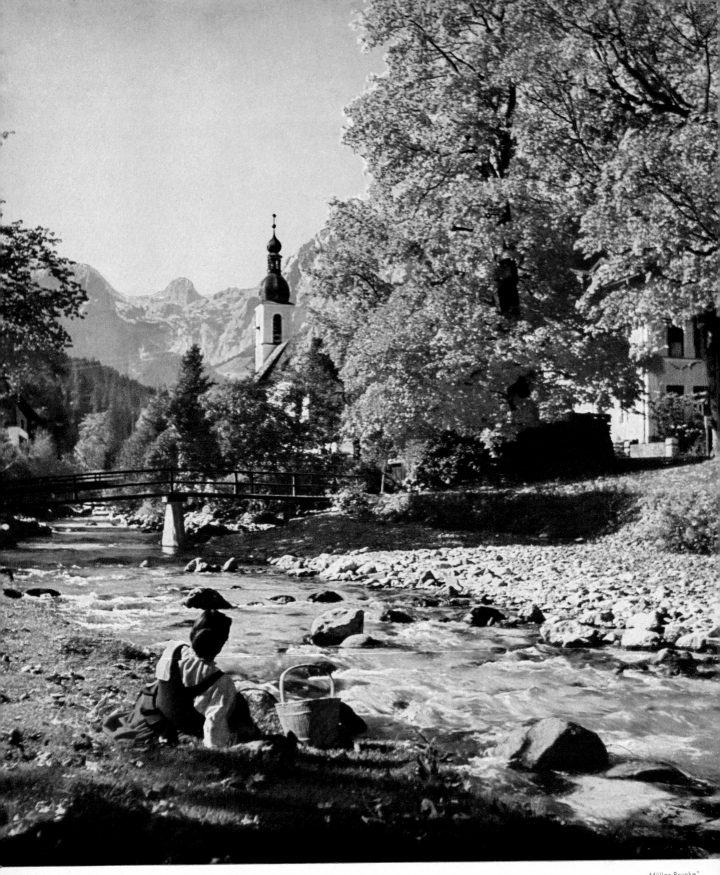

Müller-Brunke

Herbst im Berchtesgadener Land: Das Kirchlein in der Ramsau.

Fall in the Berchtesgaden area: the little church in the Ramsau.

Automne dans la contrée de Berchtesgaden: La petite église de la Ramsau.

Beautiful
BAVARIA

A VOLUME OF 160 PICTURE PAGES

WITH AN INTRODUCTION BY

JOHANN LACHNER

PICTURE CAPTIONS BY

HARALD BUSCH

UMSCHAU VERLAG · FRANKFURT AM MAIN

FIFTH EDITION

EDITORS: DR. HARALD BUSCH AND DR. H. BREIDENSTEIN.
JACKET DESIGN BY HANS BREIDENSTEIN, FRANKFURT/MAIN.

PRINTED AND BOUND BY
BRÖNNERS DRUCKEREI (BREIDENSTEIN), FRANKFURT/MAIN

THE WHOLE OF BAVARIA...

. . . in one volume: What a host of pictures! Bavaria is not what many visitors from Germany and abroad imagine it to be – a jagged outline of mountains against the sky, rocks, ski-slopes, châlets re-echoing to the strains of yodelling, wildly echoing gorges, blue lakes, magnificent royal castles . . . . and as a starting point, Munich with the towers of the Frauenkirche, its bells, its hostelries, Hofbräuhaus, carnival, and Oktoberfest. No, Bavaria is something more than this popular conception. It stretches from the mountains, across the wide Danube plain to the age-old Spessart forest and to the granite Fichtel mountains. The charm of the Alpine foothills, the austerity of the Franconian Jura, the dreaminess of little Franconian towns along the Main, the impressiveness of medieval Regensburg, the Renaissance brilliance and melancholy Gothic of busy, enterprising towns like Augsburg and Nuremberg, all are to be found in Bavaria.

And what of the old episcopal seat of Würzburg, the imperial splendour of Bamberg, the small manors and monasteries, the southern charm of the towns along the Inn, the Bavarian Forest with its tangled undergrowth, the tender frivolity of the parks at Veithöchheim or Nymphenburg? Not to mention centres of pilgrimage, Allgäu meadows, or countless river valleys – the lovely Altmühl, Isar, Lech, the majestic green-tinged Inn and the dark, sluggish Ilz. The Main is the only big river which turns its face westwards; the Danube enters Bavaria as a lively stream only to leave it with an international mission. Reader, when looking through this book, don't linger only over the familiar sights: look for the less well-known, unsuspected beauties of Bavaria.

The country which speaks to us through the pages of this book owes its creation to the grace of Napoleon; and yet the union of Swabian and Franconian territory with the core of Bavaria, which had been ruled for over a thousand years by native dukes, turned out to be a sound, reasonable rather than a violent measure. At any rate, the Wittelsbach line who governed as kings from 1806 managed to unite the three territories permanently, taking advantage of the cultural and economic ties which had bound them for centuries; so effectively were the territories welded together that Bavaria was able to survive the second world war as a natural unit (the Rhenish Palatinate excepted).

Old Bavaria, the nucleus of Bavaria, is a remarkable historical phenomenon. Populated in the sixth century by the Bajuvars, a Bohemian tribe, it comprised the present districts of Upper and Lower Bavaria. For almost fifteen hundred years the duchy and electorate of Bavaria held its own, until finally it established itself as a kingdom, incorporating parts of Franconia and Swabia. Old Bavaria has once been termed the constant pentagon of German history because its frontiers, along the Alps and Lech, down the Danube to the Bavarian Forest and up the Inn, form this shape and because all its rulers, the Agilofingers, the Luitpoldingers, and their descendants the Wittelsbachers, and even interim rulers set up by the grace of the Emperor followed a consistent policy: tradition was to be preserved and defended against outside interference. Even today people smile about the proverbial stubborn conservatism of the Bavarian. It is true that the Bajuvars made inroads South and East, but, being unable to hold the territory, were forced to retire to their "pentagon". There were times, however, when the Bavarians could not be treated as a joke, as for instance when the Elector Maximilian of Bavaria emerged as a leading figure in the Thirty Years War, determining the overwhelming Catholic character of S. Germany, or when Count Montgelas in the early days of the kingdom drew up the first liberal constitution in Germany. Old Bavaria is still difficult to understand if you are an outsider. You feel its paradoxal charm, containing generosity and stubbornness at the same time, but it remains something of an enigma. In any case, you almost feel tempted to designate Old Bavaria as the oldest of still-existing miniature states in the world, in view of its history and its importance to the country.

The Old Bavarian is essentially still a countryman. Even in the city of Munich there is a smack of the country in the air, not only at the Oktoberfest and the many fairs and markets. The intimate relationship between most town-dwellers and the country is not to be broken up. With the exception of the capital Munich and the still older imperial seat of Regensburg, there is no real "town" between the plateau and the Danube valley. However many inhabitants they may have, the country towns of Old Bavaria are really nothing but centres for the purchase of farm-requisites and markets for the sale of farm-produce. Up to a hundred years ago the Marienplatz in Munich was called "Schrannenplatz", farmers piling up the sacks of corn they brought for sale once or twice a week behind "Schrannen" (stalls). The same thing can be seen in most of the towns, particularly in the wide high streets of the Lower Bavarian towns (e. g. Landshut), or in Dingolfing, Landau, Plattling, Vilsbiburg, where an inn-lined square in the centre of the town provides accommodation for man, beast, cart and load. Civic pride growing out of the struggle against secular and spiritual lords is to be found in the Franconian parts of Bavaria. Magnificent examples of independent towns can be seen on the way from Kempten via Memmingen and Augsburg to Nuremberg and on the Main. This trait is, however, most marked in the Swabian – Franconian border district: Nördlingen, Dinkelsbühl, Rothenburg. Here the town hall and not the "Schrannenplatz" is the centre of life and the Emperor often fostered the independent spirit of the citizens in the struggle against troublesome princes by granting the title "free imperial city".

Thus the character of a town is determined by the citizens' attitude to life. Over and above its qualities as a court capital, its new "skyscrapers", its artistic pretensions, Munich will always remain the town of enjoyment, Nuremberg an industrial town *although*, not *because* its historical old part has been destroyed (the charming old buildings were a magnificent proof of the skill and industry of former craftsmen). Architecturally Würzburg is an expression of the absolute will of the Schönborn family (Prince-Bishops). Augsburg represents the enterprise of the Fugger family right down to the present day. There are many delicate nuances to be seized in the style of town houses and great differences to be seen in country houses. The rectangle of buildings which the average farmer in the Lower Bavarian valley of the Rott possesses is a palace compared with the clay building of his most important colleague in the Central Franconian Jura; the outhouse of a farm in the foothills of Upper Bavaria is a work of art compared with an Upper Franconian farm.

Let us indicate something of the character of the three races which make up Bavaria. The Old Bavarians are traditionally Catholic, given to dignified ceremonial, without being fanatics in this or any other respect; they are artistically gifted (the Upper Bavarian is jollier, more theatrical, the Lower Bavarian stiffer, more subdued). The Franconians are split by religion (Central Franconia Protestant, Lower Franconia Catholic, Upper Franconia varying according to the region); they are more far-sighted, quick-witted and industrious. The Upper Swabians, of Bavaria, predominantly Catholic, are, like all Swabians, a singular mixture of homeliness, ingenuity, sly thrift and enterprise. In the government and Civil Service of Bavaria, the Old Bavarians play the forceful, dominant rôle, the Franconians carry their point without making much ado, the Swabians maintain an ironical detachment towards politics. And yet it is the Old Bavarians who are the most tactful of the three. Old Bavaria having been a political and cultural entity for almost fifteen hundred years, it is no wonder that the Old Bavarians are able to accomplish their surprising deeds against the will, so the speak, and yet to the accompaniment of the indulgent laughter of other German countries. They manage to get what they want by apparent play-acting. But what seems unreal is real, the force behind it being genuine.

All this must be pointed out to our reader, although it does not bear directly on the pictures. Before giving oneself up to the enjoyment of Bavaria's external charm, some light should be thrown on the various elements – Celtic, Germanic and Latin, – that go to make it. And now we should like to explain quite clearly how Bavaria should be visited. The holiday crowds are attracted to the Alps, and most new-comers to Munich make straight for the Hofbräuhaus. Nothing wrong with paying homage to the accepted representative sights! In the garden or near the self-service bar of the Hofbräuhaus you easily make the acquaintance of Bavarian townsfolk, self-possessed, neither ambitious nor keen but experienced; the conversation is commonplace, tactful, restrained like that round an English fireside; it doesn't go very deep. The peaks and valleys of the Alps are more difficult proposition; they are well worth seeing, but it is better to wait until Spring or Autumn before the season is in full swing. Then, even at definite tourist resorts such as Garmisch, Berchtesgaden or Oberstdorf, you may discover while walking along a quiet path reason for their fame – the indestructible magnificence and grandeur of the Allgäu mountains, the Wetterstein and Karwendel and the so-called Salzburg Alps. You can even discover it during the season, during the summer holidays, if you are able to think for yourself and to take a few steps away from the beaten track into Alpine solitude.

And now a few words about the so-called "unknown Bavaria" – usually confined to certain Baroque churches, local festivals, romantic medieval townships, not so "unknown" after all! Not that we wish to disparage these places. Special attention might be paid, however, to the Bavarian and Bohemian Forests, sinister, deserted, vast hunting-grounds, balm to frayed nerves. Then there is the lower Main meandering through pleasent little wine-towns radiating a reflective gaiety different from the exuberance of the Moselle; the Danube plain around Straubing and the Rott valley, both an expression of the settled character of the Old Bavarian; the busy centres of the Franconian Jura and Nuremberg; the radish, asparagus and hop-growing regions around Ingolstadt, Pfaffenhofen, Schrobenhausen, Donauwörth. And how fine it is to drive through the Hollertau at harvest-time when the brightly-dressed hop-pickers are hidden beneath a forest of green tendrils!

Well-known Bavaria? It is as little-known as the part we have just been describing. Of all the hundreds of thousands of trippers bound for Ludwig II's mock castle on the Herreninsel (Chiemsee) hardly one enjoys the exquisite solitude of the woodland paths leading to the southern slope of the island. Who has visited the famous Baroque churches of Altmünster, Rott-on-Inn, Weltenburg, the towns of Amberg, Eichstätt, Passau, Burghausen, Landshut, or Moosburg? Nobody. No one finds it worthwhile to mount the cathedral hill at Freising, for centuries a great spiritual centre in Old Bavaria; no one bothers about the quaint town of Anger in Chiemgau, about the Glonn, Regnitz, Nab, Altmühl valleys, or even about the famous Isar valley near Wolfratshausen. Bavaria, the tourist centre par excellence is simply too well-known for people to want to make a closer acquaintance.

The most beautiful German town is beyond all doubt Bamberg. It is undamaged, has a thousand year past and is the only place where the best Baroque residential districts are to be found alongside a medieval imperial cathedral. One of the most beautiful stretches of countryside is to be found in the foothills of the Bavarian Alps. Compared with its rather overestimated counterpart in the South, the foothills of the Italian Alps, rather lacking in charm, or even with some delightful hilly districts, – part of Vermont (USA) for instance, or age-old Tuscany – the Bavarian foothills seem the next best thing to heaven on earth. In its ideal mixture of civilisation and wildness, gentleness and austerity, of southern atmosphere and northern piquancy, the scenery is incomparable. Here we have the example of a long, peaceful and fruitful communion of man with nature, one taming the other until harmony was finally achieved. The reader will find confirmation of this in many of the pictures. We are thinking particularly of the region from central Salzach and the north of the Chiemsee via Miesbach, and Tölz, Leitzach and Loisachtal to the southern tip of the Starnberger and Ammersee, where in the so-called "Pfaffenwinkel" (Diessen, Murnau, Weilheim, Rottenbuch, and Wessobrunn) a divine providence seems to watch over the earth.

Johann Lachner

OUR PHOTOGRAPHS *in alphabetical order*

E. Retzlaff

Bayrisches Dirndl. Frische Blumen am Mieder passen gut zur treubewahrten Tracht

Bavarian girl. Fresh flowers at the bodice look becoming on the costume faithfully preserved throughout the centuries

Jeune fille bavaroise. Des fleurs fraîches portées au corsage s'harmonisent avec le costume du pays, transmis soigneusement de génération en génération

Munich, lying in the
centre of a plateau
between the Danube
and the Alps,
is the capital
of Bavaria.
In the foreground:
Ludwigstrasse.

*Munich, situé au
milieu d'un plateau qui
s'étend du Danube aux
Alpes, est la capitale
de la Bavière.
Au premier plan:
Ludwigstrasse.*

Angermayer

auptstadt und pulsendes Herz Bayerns ist München, das mitten auf der Hochebene zwischen Donau und den Alpen liegt. Blick auf die Ludwigstraße.

München. Blick auf das in gotischen Formen erbaute Neue Rathaus (1867–1908).

Munich. A view of the new city hall built from 1867 to 1908 in Gothic style.

Munich. Vue sur le Nouvel Hôtel de Ville construit dans des formes gothiques (1867–1908).

Die Asam-Kirche Münchens in der Sendlinger Straße ist ein Kleinod eigenwillig malerischer Barockarchitektur.

The Asam Church in the Sendlinger Strasse, Munich, is a baroque gem.

L'église St. Jean Nepomucène construite par les frères Asam dans la Sendlinger Strasse, Munich, est un véritable joyau de l'art baroque.

Aufsberg

usch

Zusammen mit den klassizistisch stillen Schinkel-Bauten
und der Feldherrnhalle schließt die barocke Theatinerkirche die großzügig breite Ludwigstraße Münchens ab. (Siehe S. 2.)

A fitting end to the lavishly wide Ludwigstrasse in Munich
is provided by the Theatinerkirche and the classical buildings designed by Schinkel at Odeonsplatz. (See page 2.)

La Theatinerkirche et les bâtiments classiques conçus par Schinkel, Place de l'Odéon, forment un spectacle
digne de la grandiose Ludwigstrasse. (Voir p. 2.)

Reiter

Park im Herzen Münchens: der Englische Garten.

The "English Garden", a park in the heart of Munich.

Parc au cœur de Munich: le «Jardin Anglais».

← Angermayer

Nymphenburg, Kurfürst Max Emanuels großartige Schloßanlage bei Münche

Nymphenburg, Max Emanuel the Elector's beautifully landscaped palac

Nymphenburg, le château magnifique du Prince Electeur Max Emanue

Amann

*Das Oktoberfest auf der Theresienwiese bedeutet für München d a s Volksfest im ursprünglichen Sinne,
das hoch und niedrig, alt und jung, in ungezwungener Fröhlichkeit vereint.*

*The "Oktoberfest" is for Munich a popular festival in the literal sense of the word, bringing together old and young, rich and poor,
in an atmosphere of free and easy, hearty jollity.*

L'Oktoberfest est pour Munich une fête populaire dans le sens propre du mot, réunissant riches et pauvres, vieux et jeunes, dans une atmosphère de gaieté robuste.

8

Groth-Schmachtenberger

Was wäre der Münchner und überhaupt der Bayer ohne die Geselligkeit im Bräu bei Bier und Radi!

The Bavarian's sociability is seen at its best in the "Bräu", over beer and radishes.

Que seraient les Bavarois sans ces soirées intimes dans le «Bräu» où ils s'épanchent en goûtant la bière et les radis traditionnels?

Angermayer

Die meist geschwungene Turmhaube der Kirche ist das Wahrzeichen des bayerischen Dorfes (Rottenbuch a. d. Ammer).

The dominant feature of every Bavarian village is its bulbous church spire.

Le signe caractéristique de chaque village bavarois est le clocher en forme de bulbe.

Angermayer

Unzählige Ortschaften liegen als freundliche Akzente in der stillen weiten Ebene zwischen Alpen und Donau mit ihren vielen „Moosen" (Indersdor

The peaceful, wide moorlands of the plain between the Alps and the Danube are dotted with many pleasant little villag

Les landes larges et paisibles qui s'étalent au pied des Alpes jusqu'au Danube, sont parsemés de petits villages souriar

Schneiders

Die Backsteinkirche St. Martin in Landshut an der Isar überragt die malerischen Giebelhäuser der Hauptstadt des alten Herzogtums Niederbayern.

The brick church of St. Martin towers over the picturesque gabled houses in Landshut on the R. Isar, capital of the former duchy of Lower Bavaria.

L'église en briques de St. Martin domine les pittoresques maisons à pignon de Landshut sur Isar, capitale de l'ancien duché de la Bavière Inférieure.

12

Feierliche Messe im Dom der alten Bischofsstadt Freising.
High Mass in the cathedral of Freising, an old episcopal seat.
La grande messe célébrée dans la cathédrale de Freising, ancien siège épiscopal.

13

Burghausen an der Salzach, die Grenzstadt nach Österreich, blickt auf eine bewegte Geschichte zurück.

Burghausen on the R. Salzach, the frontier town facing Austria, looks back on stirring times.

Burghausen sur Salzach, ville de frontière qui fait face à l'Autriche, peut se vanter d'un passé mouvementé.

14

*Wasserburg is
most completely
circled by the Inn.
With its flat-roofed
houses, turrets and
arcades it has almost
southern character.*

*Les maisons
à toit plat,
les clochetons et
les galeries de
Wasserbourg
donnent à cette ville,
qu'encercle presque
entièrement l'Inn,
un air quasi
méridional.*

Wolff & Tritschler

Wasserburg, vom Inn fast völlig eingeschlossen, hat mit seinen flachen Dächern, Zinnen und Laubengängen beinahe südländischen Charakter.

Müller-Bru

Nicht weit vom Chiemsee liegt das alte Kloster Seeon.

The old monastery of Seeon lies not far from Chiemsee.

Le vieux monastère de Seeon se trouve non loin du Chiemsee.

E. Müller

Vor und in den Gebirgen Bayerns liegen zahlreiche Seen. Am bekanntesten sind die großen, wie Chiemsee, Starnberger, Ammer- und Staffelsee. Unser Bild: Der Chiemsee mit der Insel Frauenwörth und den Alpengipfeln, vom Friedhof in Gstad aus gesehen.

Many lakes dot the Bavarian mountain landscape. The best known are the larger ones such as Chiemsee, Starnberger See, Ammersee, Staffelsee. — The peaceful island of Frauenwörth in Chiemsee, with the peaks of the Alps in the background, seen from Gstad cemetery.

La partie montagneuse de la Bavière est parsemée de lacs. Les plus étendus, et par conséquent les plus connus, sont le Chiemsee, le Starnberger See, l'Ammersee, le Staffelsee. — L'île tranquille de Frauenwörth dans le Chiemsee, dominée de loin par les cimes des Alpes (vue du cimetière de Gstad).

Angermayer

Das Voralpenland mit seinen weit geschwungenen Flächen und Bergen ist eine Landschaft von eigenem Reiz.
Links der Simssee, oben das Kirchlein von Steinkirchen am Samerberg.
The foothills of the Alps have a charm of their own. Left: Simssee. Above: the little church of Steinkirchen on the Samerberg.
Les contreforts des Alpes ont un charme tout particulier. A gauche: Simssee. Au-dessus: la petite église de Steinkirchen.

Voralpenlandschaft bei Kloster Höglwörth nahe Reichenhall.

A foothills scene at Höglwörth Monastery near Reichenhall.

Paysage des contreforts des Alpes: le monastère de Höglwörth près de Reichenhall.

Angermayer

21

Baumann

Von Bad Reichenhall, das durch seine uralten Salinen und seine Jodquellen berühmt ist, führt eine Seilschwebebahn auf den Predigtstuhl.

From Bad Reichenhall, famous for its ancient salt pits and its iodine springs, a cable railway runs to the Predigtstuhl.

Un funiculaire va de Reichenhall au Predigtstuhl. Reichenhall est renommé pour ses vieilles salines et pour ses sources d'iode.

Metz

Unter den Felsenhörnern des Watzmann liegt am Zusammenfluß dreier Achen das schöne Berchtesgaden, der östlichste Punkt des deutschen Alpenlandes.

Beautiful Berchtesgaden, the most easterly point of the German Alps, lies at the confluence of three rivulets, beneath the jutting crags of the Watzmann.

23 Les rochers à pic du Watzmann surplombent Berchtesgaden, situé à l'extrémité est des Alpes Allemandes au confluent de trois ruisseaux.

Metz

Unter der steilen Watzmann-Ostwand steht malerisch am Ufer des Königssees die einsame Kapelle St. Bartholomae.

The solitary chapel of St. Bartolomae stands picturesquely on the shore of Königssee, at the foot of the steep eastern slope of the Watzmann.

La chapelle solitaire de St Bartolomae se niche au pied de la pente escarpée du Watzmann, sur la rive du Königssee.

Müller-Brunke

Das schmucke Kirchlein in der Ramsau bildet den Mittelpunkt des schon früh besiedelten Gebirgstales oberhalb Berchtesgaden.

The attractive little church in Ramsau lies at the centre of the mountain valley above Berchtesgaden. Early settlers were drawn to this spot.

Cette petite église en Ramsau se trouve au-dessus de Berchtesgaden, au creux d'une vallée montagneuse peuplée depuis des siècles.

25

Zu jeder
Jahreszeit ist das
Hochgebirge ein
unvergeßliches
Erlebnis.
Links: Winter am
Predigtstuhl.
Rechts: Sommer bei
Schwarzbachwacht.

The sight of the
mountains during
any season is
something
unforgettable.
Left: winter on
the Predigtstuhl.
Right: summer near
Schwarzbachwacht.

La vue de la
montagne
en n'importe
quelle saison est
quelque chose
d'inoubliable.
A gauche:
le Predigtstuhl
en hiver.
A droite:
les environs de
Schwarzbachwacht
en été.

← Baumann →

Der Übergang von
der schneeverwehten
Mittelspitze zur
Südspitze des
Watzmann ist
eine anspruchsvolle
Hochtour.

The passage from
the snow-swept
middle peak to the
southern peak of the
Watzmann is an
exacting
mountaineering feat.

C'est un grand exploit
d'alpiniste que de
grimper du sommet
central neigeux au
sommet sud du
Watzmann.

Baumann

Blick vom Rotpalfen
auf Hochkalter
und Nordgrat
der Blaueisspitze
mit dem
Blaueisgletscher,
dem nördlichsten
Gletscher der gesamten
Alpen.
→
View from the
Rotpalfen towards
the Hochkalter
and the northern
ridge of the
Blaueisspitze with
the Blaueis glacier,
the northernmost
of all glaciers
in the Alps.

Le Hochkalter et la
chaîne nord de la
Blaueisspitze
avec le glacier
Blaueis, vus
du Rotpalfen.

Bayrischzell liegt zu Füßen
des Aussichtsberges
Wendelstein mit seiner
Zahnradbahn.
←

Bayrischzell lies at the
foot of the Wendelstein.
A splendid view is to
be had from the top,
to which visitors are
taken by rack railway.

Bayrischzell se trouve
au pied du Wendelstein.
La montée en chemin de
fer à crémaillère vaut
la peine,
le panorama
qu'on découvre
étant exquis.

Heckmair

Reit im Winkl ist als
besonders schneereiches
Skiparadies bekannt.
→

Snow-covered
Reit im Winkl is
well-known as a
paradise for skiers.

Reit im Winkl est
bien connu en tant
que paradis de neige
pour les skieurs.

Zeitz

Schuster

Stille Berge und freundliche Kurorte säumen die Ufer des Schliersees (links) und des Tegernsees (oben).

Peaceful hills and gay little resorts line the shores of the Schliersee (left), and the Tegernsee (above).

Les rives du Schliersee (à gauche), et du Tegernsee (au-dessus), sont bordées de montagnes paisibles et de petites stations balnéaires souriantes.

H. Retzlaff

Dem einzelnstehenden Bauernhof Oberbayerns eigentümlich sind das flachgieblige, steinbeschwerte Dach und die umlaufende Galerie.

Features peculiar to the Bavarian farmhouse are the low roof weighted down with stones, and the gallery running round the upper storey.

Le toit tombant chargé de pierres et la galerie qui fait le tour de l'étage supérieur donnent à la ferme bavaroise son caractère tout spécial.

Clausing

Auch in der oberbayerischen Stadt — wie hier in Bad Tölz — ragen die flachgeneigten Dächer als Wetterschutz weit über die aneinandergedrängten Häuser vor.

In the old Bavarian towns too — as here in Bad Tölz — the flat roofs intended as a protection against the weather project over the huddled houses.

Dans les vieilles villes de Bavière, comme ici par exemple à Bad Tölz, les toits en pente défiant les intempéries surplombent les maisons serrées les unes contre les autres.

35

Angermayer

36

Angermayer

Die bayrische Tracht hat Freunde in der ganzen Welt — im Original wie in ihrer volkstümlichen Abart, dem „Dirndl" und der „Kurzen".
The Bavarian costume, attractive and at the same time practical, with the "dirndl" dress and the leather shorts, finds admirers all over the world.
Le costume bavarois, joli et pratique à la fois, avec la robe «dirndl» et la culotte de sport en cuir, trouve partout des admirateurs.

Unter der Viererspitze im Karwendel stehen noch heute die bodenständigen Häuser des alten Fuhrmanns-, Flößer- und Geigenbauerdorfes Mittenwald.

Fine stable old houses in Mittenwald, the old village of carriers, raftsmen, and violin-makers, lying beneath the Viererspitze.

De belles maisons solides à Mittenwald, vieux village de charretiers, de flotteurs de bois,
et de fabricants de violons, situé à l'ombre du Viererspitze.

38

Beckert

Der älteste Teil Partenkirchens unter dem Wettersteinmassiv ist der Floriansplatz. Über ihn führte einst die große Nord-Süd-Handelsstraße zum Brenner.
The Floriansplatz is the oldest part of Partenkirchen, at the foot of the Wetterstein. The great North-South Trade Route to the Brenner Pass once crossed this square.
La Floriansplatz, située au pied du Wetterstein, est la partie la plus vieille de Partenkirchen.
Autrefois la grande route commerciale du Brenner croisait cette place.

Die Zugspitze (2963 m) im Wettersteingebirge (vorangehende Doppelseite, Aufn. Bayer. Flugdienst) ist Deutschlands höchster Berg.
Hier wurde 1897 als Wetterstation das Münchner Haus (oben) errichtet.

The Zugspitze (9,802 feet) in the Wetterstein mountains (preceding two pages) is Germany's highest mountain.
In 1897, the "Munich House" (above) was erected there as a weather station.

La Zugspitze (2963 m) dans le massif du Wetterstein (double page précédente) est la montagne la plus élevée d'Allemagne.
C'est ici que fut construite en 1897 la «Maison de Munich» comme station météorologique.

42

Angermayer

Neujahrsmorgen über dem Wetterstein (links: die Alpspitze, rechts: die Zugspitze).
New Year's morning over the Wetterstein. Left: the Alpspitze. Right: the Zugspitze.
Le Jour de l'An au Wetterstein. A gauche: l'Alpspitze. A droite: le Zugspitze.

43

Angermayer

Bayerischer Flugdienst

*Bei Garmisch-Partenkirchen liegt der Eibsee unter den Waxensteinen (im Bild)
und der Zugspitze.*

*The Eibsee lies at the foot of the Waxenstein (above) and the Zugspitze,
near Garmisch-Partenkirchen.*

*L'Eibsee se trouve au pied du Waxenstein (au-dessus) et du Zugspitze,
près de Garmisch-Partenkirchen.*

*Der Walchensee ist mit dem 200 m tiefer liegenden Kochelsee
durch die Anlagen eines großen Kraftwerks verbunden.*

*The difference in altitude between Walchensee and Kochelsee,
600 ft., is used to generate electric power.*

*Le lac de Walchen est relié au lac de Kochel, situé 200 m. plus bas,
par les conduites d'une centrale hydroélectrique.*

44

Klammet

Die Partnachklamm ist eine tiefe, enge Felsenschlucht, durch die sich die Gebirgsbäche in Jahrtausenden den Weg zu Tal gewaschen haben.

The Partnachklamm is a deep narrow ravine washed by mountain-streams cutting their way into the valley.

Le Partnachklamm est une gorge étroite et profonde lavée par des ruisseaux de montagne qui se frayent un passage jusqu'à la vallée.

46

Gesell

Bis hoch hinauf ist das Gebirge reich an kleinen Seen, die wie Augen der Erde den Himmel spiegeln. Der Wagenbrüch-See mit dem Karwendel.
Even the mountain heights abound with small lakes reflecting sky and earth. The Wagenbrüch-See with the Karwendel in the distance.
Même la haute montagne abonde en petits lacs qui reflètent ciel et terre. Le Wagenbrüch-See; au fond le Karwendel.

Kronburger

Clausing
→

Kloster Ettal, ein bedeutendes Baudenkmal, ist als Wallfahrtsort
durch sein Gnadenbild berühmt.

*Ettal monastery, an important architectural work, is famous for its
miraculous image, attracting pilgrims.*

*Le monastère d'Ettal, important monument, est connu par
son image miraculeuse qui attire tant de pèlerins.*

Oberammergau unter dem Kofel wurde durch die Passionsspiele
und durch seine Bildschnitzer zu einem Begriff in der ganzen Welt.

*Oberammergau has a special significance throughout the world
on account of its Passion Play and its wood-carvers.*

*Le nom d'Oberammergau a pris une signification toute particulière dans
le monde à cause des sculpteurs sur bois et du Mystère de la Passion.*

Autsberg

Schloß Herrenchiemsee (1878–1885). Blick aus dem Friedenssaal in den dem Versailler Schloß nachempfundenen Spiegelsaal.

Herrenchiemsee castle (1878–1885). A view from the "Hall of Peace" into the "Hall of Mirrors", modelled after that of the Palace of Versailles.

Château d'Herrenchiemsee (1878–1885). Vue prise de la « Salle de la Paix » sur la «Galerie des Glaces » imitée de Versailles.

Aufsberg

*Die um 1870 durch König Ludwig II. von Bayern im nachempfundenen Stil erbauten „Königsschlösser" Herrenchiemsee (links), Linderhof (oben)
und Neuschwanstein (S. 55) sind das Ziel vieler Reisegesellschaften.*

The royal palaces of Herrenchiemsee (left), Linderhof (above), and Neuschwanstein (p. 55), erected c. 1870 by King Ludwig II of Bavaria, attract many tourists.

*Les palais royaux de Herrenchiemsee (à gauche),
Linderhof (au-dessus), et Neuschwanstein (p. 55), érigés par le roi Louis II de Bavière vers 1870, attirent beaucoup de touristes.*

51

Rinold

Klöster und Kirchen, Kapellen und Bildstöcke, malerisch der Landschaft eingefügt, geben Bayern vielfach das Gepräge. St. Koloman im Schwangau bei Füssen.

Monasteries and churches, chapels and wayside images fitting picturesquely into the countryside impart to Bavaria its special character. St. Koloman near Füssen.

Monastères, statues de saints au bord du chemin, églises et chapelles qui s'adaptent harmonieusement au paysage donnent à la Bavière son caractère tout à fait spécial.

Schmidt-Glaßner

Die kleine Wallfahrtskirche „In der Wies" bei Steingaden ist einer der großartigsten Kirchenbauten des abendländischen Spätbarock.
The small church "In der Wies" near Steingaden is one of the most magnificent constructions of the late Baroque period, attracting many pilgrims.
La petite église « In der Wies » près de Steingaden est un des édifices les plus magnifiques datant des dernières années de l'époque baroque.

Arnold

Arnold →

Über Füssen am Lech thront das Hohe Schloß,
einst Sommerresidenz der Augsburger Fürstbischöfe.

The Hohe Schloss, once the summer residence of the prince-bishops
of Augsburg stands above the town of Füssen.

Le Hohe Schloss, ancienne résidence des princes-évêques d'Augsbourg,
domine la ville de Füssen.

Auf schroffem Fels errichtet, erhebt sich Neuschwanstein,
ein steingewordener königlicher Traum vom Mittelalter.

Dramatically perched on a high rock, Neuschwanstein is a
19th century realisation of a fairy-tale castle.

Neuschwanstein, qui se dresse sur un rocher escarpé,
est un château de fées construit au 19e siècle.

*Das Luftbild
verdeutlicht die
einzigartige Lage
Oberstdorfs zu Füßen
der Allgäuer Alpen.*

*This aerial view shows
the unique location
of Oberstdorf at the
base of the Allgäu Alps.*

*La vue aérienne rend
sensible la situation
magnifique d'Oberstdorf
au pied des Alpes
de l'Allgäu.*

Albrecht Brugger

Aufsberg

Das reizende Bad Oberdorf bei Hindelang im Ostrachtal des Allgäus, von der Straße zum Oberjoch aus, die nach Reutte in Tirol führt.

Charming Bad Oberdorf near Hindelang in the Ostrachtal seen from the road leading up the Oberjoch to Reutte in the Tyrol.

La charmante petite ville de Bad Oberdorf dans l'Ostrachtal, vue de la route d'Oberjoch (menant à Reutte en Tyrol).

Metz

Zu Füßen der mächtigen Berge des grünen Allgäu liegt das vielbesuchte Oberstdorf. Im Hintergrund: der Kratzer.

At the foot of the huge mountains of green Allgäu lies Oberstdorf, a tourist haunt. In the background: the Kratzer.

Oberstdorf, lieu bien fréquenté par les villégiateurs, se trouve au pied des vastes montagnes de l'Allgäu verte. Au fond le Kratzer.

Windstoßer

← Baumann

Von solchem Pulverschnee träumt jeder Skifahrer.

Such snow is the dream of every skier.

Une neige pareille, c'est le rêve de tout skieur!

Die Schneemulden unter dem Nebelhorn (2224 m) bei Oberstdorf, ein Skiparadies,
sind durch eine Seilschwebebahn bequem zu erreichen.
An klaren Tagen leuchten über der Höffats (im Hintergrund rechts) die Ötztaler Berge.

*The snowy slopes below the Nebelhorn (7295 ft.), a skiers' paradise near Oberstdorf,
are easily to be reached by means of a cable railway.
On clear days you can see the Oetztaler Mountains gleaming above the Höffats (right).*

*Les pentes neigeuses au-dessus du Nebelhorn (2224 m.) ont été mises à la portée
des skieurs par un funiculaire. Par temps clair on peut
voir scintiller les Alpes d'Oetztal qui dominent les Höffats (a droite).*

Aufsberg

Aus der kargen Felswirklichkeit bei Einödsbach, dem südlichsten bewohnten Punkt Bayerns
und Deutschlands, zaubert der Winterreif eine Märchenwelt.
Über dem Bachertal (v. l. n. r.) die Trettachspitze, Mädelegabel, Hochfrottspitze und Bockkarkopf. →

The harsh, barren crags near Einödsbach, the southernmost inhabited hamlet of Bavaria and
of Germany, are transformed by the hoar frost into a wonderworld. The Trettachspitze,
Mädelegabel, Hochfrottspitze and Bockkarkopf rising over the Bachertal.

Le givre transforme en un monde féerique les rochers durs et arides près d'Einödsbach à l'extrémité
sud de la Bavière et de l'Allemagne. Le Trettachspitze, Mädelegabel, Hochfrottspitze,
et Bockkarkopf qui dominent le Bachertal.

Bei einer Alp in den Bergen um Einödsbach.

Alpine pastures near Einödsbach.

Pâturage alpestre près d'Einödsbach.

Aufsberg

Der Große Alpsee bei Immenstadt inmitten des Allgäu mit dem Blick auf Bühl.

The Grosse Alpsee near Immenstadt in the heart of the Allgäu, looking towards Bühl.

Le Grosse Alpsee près d'Immenstadt au cœur de l'Allgäu. Au fond: Bühl.

Bischofberger

Über den Bergen im Allgäu thront als ihr stolzester der Hochvogel (2596 m).

The Hochvogel peak rises proudly above all others in the Allgäu (8507 ft.).

La cime fière du Hochvogel domine toutes celles de l'Allgäu (2596 m).

65

Strähle

←

Der bayerische Löwe auf dem Molenkopf der Hafeneinfahrt von Lindau zeigt an,
daß dieser Zipfel Landes im Bodensee zu Bayern gehört.

The lion of Bavaria on the pierhead at the entrance to Lindau harbour indicates
that this tip of Germany's largest inland lake belongs to Bavaria.

Le lion de Bavière qui orne la pointe de la jetée à l'entrée du port de Lindau
indique qu'un coin du Bodensee, le plus grand lac de l'Allemagne,
appartient à la Bavière.

Der größte der Voralpenseen ist der Bodensee, das „Schwäbische Meer",
mit Lindau, der hübschen „Ferieninsel".

The largest of the lakes before the Alps, is the Bodensee,
called "Schwäbisches Meer", with Lindau, the pretty
"holiday island".

Le lac le plus important devant les Alpes, est le Bodensee,
surnommé «Schwäbisches Meer», avec Lindau «l'île de villégiature».

Aufsberg

Fürstabt Anselm I. ließ zwischen 1734 und 1742 die Innenräume seiner Residenz in Kempten im Allgäu überaus prächtig ausgestalten.

Anselm I, the prince abbot, had his residence in Kempten splendidly decorated from 1734 to 1742.

Le prince abbé Anselme 1er, entre 1734 et 1742, fit décorer d'une façon splendide en tous points l'intérieur de sa résidence à Kempten dans l'Allgäu.

Aufsberg

Schwäbische Biederkeit offenbart der Marktplatz von Kempten, dem Mittelpunkt des Allgäus, dieses Landes der Milchwirtschaft.

Kempten market place the good honest solidity of the Swabians. This township lies in the heart of the Allgäu, a rich dairy-farming region.

Ici, sur la place du marché de Kempten, tout respire la franchise souabe. Cette commune se trouve dans le centre de l'Allgäu,
région prospère à l'industrie laitière.

69

Mutter

In der Lechstadt Landsberg ist, zumal um den Platz beim Schmalzturm, noch Wesentliches vom alten Stadtbild erhalten.

The essential character of old Landsberg on the Lech has been retained, at least around the square in front of the Schmalzturm.

Le caractère propre à la vieille ville de Landsberg s/Lech a été conservé au moins dans le quartier autour de la place du Schmalzturm.

Busch

Auch in dem schönen Rathaus zu Memmingen zeigt sich die ausgesprochene Kunstbegabung
des Volksstammes der Schwaben, die ganz Süddeutschland befruchtete.

The Swabians' marked artistic talent which benefited the whole of S. Germany is shown in the beautiful townhall of Memmingen.

71 *L'hôtel de ville de Memmingen ainsi que beaucoup d'autres édifices parsemés dans toute l'Allemagne du Sud est un témoin du talent artistique des Souabes.*

Die mächtige Klosterkirche von Ottobeuren ist die Krone des schwäbischen Barock.

The huge church of Ottobeuren monastery is a gem of Swabian Baroque.

Le vaste monastère d'Ottobeuren est un joyau de l'architecture baroque souabe.

72

Schmidt-Glaßner

Feierliche Ruhe erfüllt den streng geformten Kirchenraum von Ottobeuren.
Aber die klare Gliederung wird überspielt durch die lebendige Fülle der plastischen und der malerischen Ausstattung.

Ottobeuren. A solemn stillness pervades the strict forms of the church interior, softened by the vived architectural decoration.

Ottobeuren. Les formes sévères de l'intérieur, qu'adoucit une profusion d'ornements chatoyants, degagent un air de paix solennelle.

Selbst die kleineren, weniger bekannten Kirchen Süddeutschlands
sind oft reich an Kunstschätzen und malerischen Winkeln.
Seitenkapelle der Kollegiatkirche Mindelheim.

Even the smaller, less famous churches of S. Germany are often rich
in art treasures and picturesque corners.
Side chapel at the collegiate church of Mindelheim.

Même les églises moins connues de l'Allemagne du Sud sont souvent
riches en trésors artistiques et en détails pittoresques. Chapelle dans l'église
collégiale de Mindelheim.

In St. Ulrich und Afra zu Augsburg, der Hauptstadt Oberschwabens,
ruhen die Mitglieder der Familie Fugger, der berühmten, einstmals die Welt
beherrschenden Unternehmerkaufleute dieser bedeutenden Handelsstadt.

The tombs of the Fugger family, once famous bankers with the world at
their feet, lie in the church of SS. Ulrich and Afra at Augsburg,
an important commercial centre.

Les tombeaux de la famille Fugger, banquiers d'une renommée mondiale qui
tenaient autrefois les ficelles de la haute finance, se trouvent dans l'église
des Saints Ulrich et Afra à Augsbourg, centre commercial important.

Jeiter

Augsburg mit seiner breiten Maximilianstraße besitzt besonders schöne alte Brunnen. Der Herkules-Brunnen (1610) und der Turm St. Ulrich und Afra.

Augsburg with its square-like Maximilianstrasse possesses especially fine old fountains. The Hercules Fountain (1610) and the spire of SS. Ulrich and Afra.

Augsbourg avec la Maximilianstrasse, si large qu'elle ressemble à une place, possède de vieilles fontaines d'une beauté exceptionnelle.
La Fontaine d'Hercule (1610) et la flèche de l'église des Saints Ulrich et Afra.

Schneiders

Augsburg, die traditionsreiche Hauptstadt Oberschwabens. Blick in die Maximilanstraße, im Hintergrund Rathaus und Dom.

Augsburg, the capital of Upper Swabia, is full of traditions. Our picture: Maximilianstrasse with townhall and cathedral as a backdrop.

Augsbourg est la vieille capitale de la Haute Souabe. Maximilianstrasse avec, en arrière,
l'hôtel de ville et la cathédrale.

Schmidt-Glaßner

Günzburg an der Donau, ein reizendes Städtchen, ist insbesondere wegen seines Renaissanceschlosses und seiner Frauenkirche besuchenswert.

Günzburg on the Danube, a charming little town noteworthy for its Renaissance palace and the Frauenkirche (Church of Our Lady).

Günzburg sur Danube, charmante petite ville dont le palais renaissance et la Frauenkirche (Notre Dame) sont dignes d'attention.

78

Der sogenannte Schimmelturm in Lauingen a. d. Donau, das wie Günzburg lange Zeit hindurch Residenz war.

The so-called Schimmelturm (White Horse Tower) in Lauingen on the Danube, like Günzburg once a seat of nobility.

La Schimmelturm (tour dite « du Cheval Blanc ») à Lauingen sur Danube, qui comme Günzburg, était une résidence seigneuriale.

*Neuburg ragt
...rt über der
...nau das mächtige
...loß der Herzöge
...n Pfalz-Neuburg
...estflügel
...1 1530).*

*...uburg.
...e huge palace
...the dukes
...Pfalz-Neuburg
...est wing c. 1530)
...ectly overlooks
...e Danube.*

*...ubourg.
...vaste palais
...s ducs de
...alz-Neubourg
...ont l'aile ouest
...te d'environ 1530)
...mine le Danube.*

—

...midt-Glaßner

*Das Mortuarium
des Domes
der alten
Bischofsstadt
Eichstätt.*

*The mortuary
chapel in the
cathedral of
Eichstätt, an old
episcopal centre.*

*La chapelle
mortuaire
de la cathédrale
d'Eichstätt,
ancien siège
d'évêque.*

Wolff & Tritschler

81

Saebens

Bei Neuburg. Die feuchten Niederungen von Moos und Ried
begleiten auf weiten Strecken den Lauf der Donau.   Im Donauried.

Starting from Neuburg, the Danube flows through flat, sometimes boggy country.   The marshlands of the Donauried.

A partir de Neubourg, le Danube coule à travers une plaine humide et marécageuse.   Les terrains marécageux du Donauried.

Lauterwasser

*Die mächtige Anlage der Harburg über dem engen Durchbruch der aus
Franken kommenden Wörnitz zur Donau hin.
Sie beherrschte einst die wichtige Handelsstraße, die von Italien über
den Brenner und Augsburg zum Norden führte.*

*The great castle of Harburg high above the Wörnitz formerly guarded
the important trade route leading northwards from Italy over the Brenner Pass.*

*Le château grandiose d'Harbourg qui surplombe le Wornitz veillait autrefois
sur l'ancienne route commerciale qui, traversant le Col du Brenner,
reliait l'Italie avec le nord.*

Saebens
→

*Wo die Wörnitz in die Donau einmündet, liegt das ehemalige
Reichsstädtchen Donauwörth mit seinem Färbertor.*

*At the confluence of the Wörnitz and the Danube lies the former free
imperial city of Donauwörth with its Färbertor.*

*Au confluent du Wornitz et du Danube se trouve l'ancienne ville libre
de Donauworth avec sa Färbertor.*

Strache

Das tausendjährige Berching liegt verträumt im oberpfälzischen Jura beim Ludwigskanal, der seit über hundert Jahren den Main mit der Donau, die Nordsee mit dem Schwarzen Meer verbindet.

Berching, with its thousand years of history, lies dreamily in the hills of the Upper Palatinate, near the Ludwigskanal which has been a connecting link between Main and Danube, North Sea and Black Sea, for over a hundred years.

La petite ville millénaire de Berching sommeille dans les collines du Haut Palatinat près du Ludwigskanal, lien qui rattache depuis plus d'une centaine d'années le Mein avec le Danube, la Mer du Nord avec la Mer Noire.

Schmidt-Glaßner

Wahrzeichen der alten bayerischen Herzogsresidenz Ingolstadt a. d. Donau sind die mächtigen Backsteintürme der Frauenkirche und die Tore der alten Stadtmauer.
Landmarks of the old Bavarian ducal seat of Ingolstadt on the Danube are the great brick towers of the Frauenkirche and the gates of the old town ramparts.
Les grandes tours de la Frauenkirche et les portes des vieux remparts de la ville sont symboles de la résidence ducale d'Ingolstadt sur Danube.

Schmidt-Glaßner

Burg Randeck
im Altmühltal.

Randeck Castle
overlooking
the valley of
the Altmühl.

Le château
de Randeck qui
commande
le vallon
d'Altmuhl.

→

Gundermann

Die gewaltigen Steintore des Donaudurchbruchs durch die Kalkfelsen des Jura bei Kelheim.

The Danube cuts its way through the impressive chalk cliffs of the Franconian Jura near Kelheim.

Le Danube se fraye un chemin à travers les impressionnants rochers calcaires du Jura Franconien près de Kelheim.

Inmitten der romantischen Felseneinsamkeit des Donaudurchbruchs bei Kelheim liegt das Benediktiner-Kloster Weltenburg.
Der Bau ist eine Schöpfung der Münchner Brüder Asam.

The Benedictine monastery of Weltenburg, a creation of the brothers Asam, lies romantically amid the deserted cliffs near Kelheim.

Le monastère Bénédictin de Weltenbourg, œuvre des frères Asam, se niche pittoresquement parmi les rochers solitaires près de Kelheim.

Hege

In goldener Rüstung auf silbernem Roß scheint der Ritter Georg vom Himmel herab in den Kirchenraum von Weltenburg zu reiten.

Clad in golden armour and mounted on a silver horse, St. George seems to be riding straight from heaven into the church of Weltenburg.

Armé en or de pied en cap et monté sur un coursier en argent, St. Georges, descendu directement du ciel, semble traverser l'église de Weltenbourg en coup de vent.

Jenseits der alten Donaubrücke (um 1140) erhebt sich das 2000jährige Regensburg, reich an Denkmälern einer bedeutenden Vergangenheit.

The venerable city of Regensburg, rich in monuments to its impressive past of 2000 years, lies beyond the old Danube Bridge (c. 1140).

La vénérable ville de Ratisbonne, riche en monuments à son passé mouvementé, est située au-delà du vieux Pont du Danube (vers 1140).

92

Schmidt-Glaßner

Im Saal des Regensburger Rathauses tagte von 1663 bis 1806 der „Immerwährende Reichstag", das erste Parlament des alten Deutschen Reiches.

In the hall of Regensburg townhall, the "Perpetual Diet", an imperial assembly consisting of representatives of the principalities and towns, met from 1663–1806.

Dans la grande salle de l'hôtel de ville de Ratisbonne siégea de 1663 à 1806 la «Diète Perpétuelle», assemblée impériale de représentants des Etats.

93

Hase

Viele süddeutsche Städte besitzen noch immer Mauern, Tore und Türme aus alter Zeit. Das Ellinger Tor in Weißenburg.

Many South German towns still possess the ramparts, gates, and towers of former days. The Ellinger Gate in Weissenburg.

Mainte ville de l'Allemagne du Sud possède toujours les remparts, portes, et tours d'autrefois. La Porte d'Ellingen à Weissenbourg.

94

Busch

Noch wie in alter Zeit fahren Bauernwagen durch die Tore vieler alter Marktstädtchen. Das Spitaltor in Rothenburg o. d. Tauber.

Just as in the past, farm cars still drive through the gates of many an old market town. The Hospital Gate at Rothenburg.

Comme dans le passé, des charettes de paysans roulent toujours sous les portes de mainte petite ville de campagne. La Porte de l'Hôpital à Rothenburg.

95

Strähle

E. Retzlaff
→

*Wie aus der Spielzeugschachtel! Das einzigartige Bild der alten
schwäbischen Reichsstadt Nördlingen, wie es sich aus der Luft darbietet.*

*No toy city this — but the unique aerial view of Nördlingen,
the old Swabian free imperial city.*

*Il ne s'agit pas ici d'une ville-jouet, mais de Nordlingen,
vieille ville libre souabe (vue à vol d'oiseau).*

*Nördlingen. Malerisch scharen sich Rathaus und andere Bauten um den Turm
der Stadtkirche St. Georg.*

*Nördlingen. A picturesque group of buildings, among them the townhall,
clusters around the tower of St. George's.*

*Nordlingen. De pittoresques édifices, dont l'hôtel de ville,
se groupent autour du clocher de l'église St. Georges.*

96/97

*Nördlingen. Der „Daniel",
der Turm der Stadtkirche
St. Georg, ragt über die
hohen Giebeldächer der
Löpsinger Straße.*

*Nördlingen. The "Daniel",
the tower on
St. George's church,
rising above the
gabled roofs of
Löpsinger Street.*

*Nördlingen. «Daniel»,
tour de l'église
S. Georges, s'élance
au-dessus des toits
élevés hérissés de pignons
de la rue de Löpsingen.*

In Nördlingen kann man noch heute auf dem alten Wehrgang die ganze Stadt umwandern. Blick aufs Löpsinger Tor.

One can still walk around the entire town of Nördlingen along its covered town wall. View of Löpsinger Gate.

A Nördlingen on peut faire le tour de toute la ville sur le vieux chemin de ronde. Vue sur la porte de Löpsingen.

Aufsberg

Dinkelsbühl. Der Gasthof „Zum Greifen", das Rothenburger Tor und das Spital in dem alten Ackerbürgerstädtchen.

The Griffin Inn, Rothenburg Gate, and hospital in Dinkelsbühl, an old market town on the Wörnitz.

L'Auberge du Griffon, la Porte de Rothenburg, et l'hôpital de Dinkelsbühl, vieux bourg situé sur le Wornitz.

100

*Der lichte Raum der Stadtkirche
St. Georg in Dinkelsbühl ist
der reifste aller Hallenkirchen-
bauten in Süddeutschland
(1448–92).*

*Light streams into St. George's
at Dinkelsbühl, the most mature
of all church buildings of its
type in S. Germany (1448–92).*

*La lumière pénètre à flots la nef
de l'église St. Georges à
Dinkelsbühl (1448–92),
qui dépasse en hardiesse
de conception tous les édifices
de son genre dans le Sud
de l'Allemagne.*

101   Busch

Schäfer aus dem Ries bei Nördlingen in altschwäbischer Tracht.

Shepherd in old Swabian costume from the Ries country near Nördlingen.

Berger portant le vieux costume souabe, du pays dit Ries près de Nordlingen.

E. Retzlaff

E. Retzlaff

Fränkische Bäuerin aus Effeltrich.
Franconian woman from Effeltrich.
Paysanne franconienne d'Effeltrich.

Landschaft in Franken. Das Taubertal mit dem Kirchlein von Dettwang, von Rothenburgs Burggarten aus gesehen.

Franconian scenery. The valley of the Tauber, and Dettwang church, seen from Rothenburg Castle gardens.

Paysage franconien. Le vallon du Tauber et l'église de Dettwang, vus du château de Rothenburg.

Busch

Busch

Über dem Taubertal das alte Reichsstädtchen Rothenburg, Inbegriff der Romantik in Deutschland. Links im Tal das Toppler-Schlößchen.

Lying high above the Tauber valley is the small town of Rothenburg, epitome of romantic Germany.

La vieille ville de Rothenburg, qui réunit tous les éléments du romantique allemand.

An der breiten Herrengasse in Rothenburg stehen zwischen Burgtor und
Rathaus reiche Patrizierhäuser aus der Renaissancezeit.

The wide Herrengasse in Rothenburg, between the Castle Gate and the townhall,
is lined with fine houses built by well-to-do burghers during the Renaissance period.

La «Herrengasse» de Rothenburg, rue très large
située entre la Porte du Château et l'hôtel de ville, est bordée de belles
maisons renaissance construites par des bourgeois prospères.

So klein erscheint die Welt
von der Höhe des Rathausturmes (links) in Rothenburg.

A pygmy world seen from the top of the townhall tower (left), Rothenburg.

Que le monde en bas paraît minuscule, vu du haut de la tour
de l'hôtel de ville (à gauche) à Rothenburg.

Baur

Einer der schönsten Winkel von Rothenburg: Das „Plönlein" mit dem Blick auf gleich zwei Stadttore.

One of the most beautiful old corners in Rothenburg: the Plönlein with a view of two of the city gates.

Un joli coin de Rothenburg: le Plonlein, dominant à la fois deux des portes de la ville.

108

Rothenburg. Der Markusturm mit dem Röderbogen, Reste einer älteren, enger gezogenen Stadtbefestigung.

Rothenburg. The Markusturm with the Röder archway, the remains of an older, shorter ring of fortifications.

Rothenburg. La Tour St. Marc avec son Arc Roeder, tout ce qui reste d'une enceinte plus ancienne et moins étendue.

Busch

→

In Rothenburg wacht vom Balkon über der Rathaus-Vorhalle
die Justitia mit Waage und Schwert.

Justice, armed with sword and scales,
watches from the balcony over the townhall vestibule in Rothenburg.

Rothenburg. Dressée sur le balcon, armée d'un épée et d'une balance,
la Justice veille sur le vestibule de l'hôtel de ville.

Das Hegereiterhaus im Hof des alten Spitals von Rothenburg.

The Hegereiterhaus in the courtyard of the old Rothenburg hospital.

La Hegereiterhaus dans la cour du vieil hôpital de Rothenburg.

11

Stürz

Sulzfeld. Malerische Orte liegen im Land der Franken, zumal am Main, dem alten Handelsweg.

Sulzfeld. Picturesque spots are to be found everywhere in Franconia, especially along the old Main trade route.

Sulzfeld. De pittoresques endroits se trouvent partout en Franconie, surtout le long de la vieille route commerciale du Mein.

Wagner

Das Rödelseertor in Iphofen, einer gut erhaltenen Kleinstadt des Mittelalters.

A Gate at Iphofen, a well-preserved medieval township.

Une porte à Iphofen, bourg médiéval en bon état de conservation.

Metz

Mit seinen Türmen und dem Mauerring bietet Marktbreit ein besonders reizvolles Stadtbild.

The towers and fortifications of Marktbreit present a specially delightful picture.

Les tours et les fortifications du bourg de Marktbreit offrent aux yeux un spectacle particulièrement charmant.

Schneiders

Schweinfurt, heute eine Industriestadt, ist stolz auf sein schönes altes Rathaus (nach 1570).

Schweinfurt, today an industrial town, is proud of its fine old townhall (post 1570).

Schweinfurt est fier de son beau vieil hôtel de ville (construit après 1570).

Saebens

Gundermann

*Die alte Brücke in Würzburg führte einst in die prächtige Stadt des Barock,
reich an ehrwürdigen Kirchen und prunkenden weltlichen Bauten. Aus dem
Ruinenfeld entstand jetzt ein neues Würzburg. (Vorkriegsbild.)*

*Würzburg. This old bridge used to lead into an old Baroque town, rich in
historic churches and magnificent secular buildings. It was transformed
into a heap of ruins, from which the new Würzburg is slowly emerging.
(Pre-war picture.)*

*Wurtzbourg. Ce vieux pont donna accès à la ville du baroque, riche en
églises vénérables et en magnifiques édifices séculaires. Tout fut transformé
en désert de ruines, d'où renaît lentement le nouveau Wurtzbourg.
(Photo d'avant-guerre.)*

*Die Bischöfe von Würzburg besaßen in der Feste Marienberg, die die Stadt
überragt, am wichtigen Mainübergang ein mächtiges Bollwerk.*

*Würzburg is the gem of all the Main towns. The mighty fortress of Marienberg,
at the Main river crossing, was the seat of the Prince Bishops of Würzburg.*

*Wurtzbourg est le joyau de toutes les villes du Mein. Le vaste bastion de
Marienberg qui garde le passage du Mein fut résidence des Princes-
Evêques de Wurtzbourg.*

117

Hallensleben

Glücklicherweise blieb in der ausgebrannten Würzburger Residenz (1719–50) wenigstens das herrliche Treppenhaus mit den Fresken des Tiepolo ...

The only part of Würzburg Palace (1719–50) untouched by the flames was this magnificent staircase by Balthasar Neumann, adorned with Tiepolo frescoes.

Ce magnifique escalier, œuvre de Balthasar Neumann (orné de fresques de Tiepolo), fut la seule partie du Palais de Wurtzbourg qu'on put soustraire aux flammes. **118**

Saebens

... blieben auch die strahlenden äußeren Formen der ganzen Architektur erhalten.

Würzburg Palace. Fortunately, the outer walls of this impressive Baroque structure are still standing. Facade overlooking the gardens.

Le Palais de Wurtzbourg. Heureusement, les murs extérieurs de cette structure impressionnante baroque existent toujours. Façade donnant sur le parc.

Baumann

Der Park des Lustschlosses Veitshöchheim bei Würzburg ist mit Gartenplastiken, Lauben und Irrgängen ein Garten des Spätbarock, des Rokoko (um 1780).

With its sculptures, arboured walks, and mazes, Veitshöchheim park is a typical example of a Rococo garden (c. 1780).

Sculptures, tonnelles, et labyrinthes, tout dans le parc de Veitshöchheim annonce le rococo (vers 1780).

Busch

Die Kindergruppen, die das Parterre des barocken Hofgartens in Würzburg abschließen, geben der festlichen Gartenfront dieses Schlosses eine heitere Note.

A merry note is supplied by the group statues of children in the formal baroque gardens at the rear of Würzburg Palace.

Le parc formel baroque derrière le Palais de Wurtzbourg dégage un air joyeux, grâce aux statues d'enfants en groupe.

Busch

Gundermann

Wie ein Bild aus alter Zeit wirkt heute noch Karlstadt am Main,
das um 1200 gegründet wurde.

Karlstadt on Main presents a picture of a by-gone age.

A Carlstadt s/Mein tout respire les jours d'antan.

Am einzigartigen Marktplatz in Miltenberg am Main stehen die Fachwerkhäuser
fast wie Kulissen aus einem Theaterspiel „Aus der alten Zeit".

The half-timbered houses of the quaint market place of Miltenberg
would make an ideal background to a play with the theme "In old days".

Quel beau décor pour une pièce jouée en costume de style,
que ces vieilles maisons à colombage du marché pittoresque de Miltenberg.

Gundermann

Einer der eindrucksvollsten Großbauten der deutschen Renaissance: das im Krieg ausgebrannte Schloß der Mainzer Erzbischöfe in Aschaffenburg am Main.

One of the most impressive structures of the German Renaissance was the palace of the Archbishops of Mainz in Aschaffenburg.

Un des édifices les plus impressionnants de la Renaissance en Allemagne fut le palais des Archevêques de Mayence à Aschaffenbourg.

In den sagenumwobenen Wäldern des Spessarts wirkt das versteckt liegende Wasserschlößchen Mespelbrunn wie ein verwunschenes Märchenschloß.

Like an enchanted fairy-tale castle in a lake, Mespelbrunn lies tucked away in the Spessart woods, home of many legends.

Relégué au fond de la Forêt du Spessart, source de tant de légendes, Mespelbrunn, véritable château de fée, se dresse au milieu d'un lac.

Busch

Auf der herben Rhön stoßen die Grenzen von Bayern, Thüringen und Hessen zusammen. Einer der stimmungsvollsten Gipfel dieses vulkanischen Berglandes ist der Kreuzberg bei Bischofsheim mit dem Kloster und seiner Golgatha-Gruppe. In der Ferne die Wasserkuppe.

The frontiers of Franconia, Thuringia, and Hesse meet on the Rhön. One of the most impressive peaks of this volcanic country is the Kreuzberg near Bischofsheim with its monastery and Golgatha group. In the distance, Wasserkuppe.

Les frontières de Franconie, de Thuringe, et d'Hesse se croisent sur le Rhoen. Une des cimes les plus impressionnantes de ce pays volcanique est le Kreuzberg, près de Bischofsheim, renommé pour son monastère et son Calvaire. Aux lointains, la Wasserkuppe.

Busch

Am Fuße der Rhönberge liegen bedeutende Kurorte, vor allem Bad Kissingen.
Steht man bei Roßbach, nicht weit von Bad Brückenau, so breitet sich weithin das Panorama der Rhönkuppen.

Many spas lie at the foot of the Rhön hills, the most important being Bad Kissingen.
From Rossbach, not far from Bad Brückenau, one has a good view of the peaks of the Rhön.

Au pied des montagnes du Rhoen se nichent bien des stations balnéaires dont la plus célèbre est Bad Kissingen.
De Rossbach, non loin de Bad Brückenau on voit scintiller les cimes du Rhoen.

Die Türme der
Wallfahrtskirche
Vierzehnheiligen
(unser Bild), denen der
Klosterkirche Banz
gegenüber, blicken weit
hinaus ins Frankenland.

The towers of the
Vierzehnheiligen
pilgrimage church
(left), opposite the
monastic church of Banz,
command a good view
of the fertile
Franconian countryside.

Les flèches de l'église
des Vierzehnheiligen
(à droite), lieu de
pèlerinage, font face à
celles de l'église
conventuelle de Banz.
Elles dominent un
paysage fertile
franconien.

→

Was Ottobeuren und
„Die Wies" für den
schwäbischen und den
bayerischen, das ist die
Wallfahrtskirche
Vierzehnheiligen
(1743–72) für den
fränkischen Spätbarock.

The pilgrimage church
of the Vierzehnheiligen
(1743–72) plays the
same rôle in
Franconian Rococo art
as Ottobeuren and
"The Wies" in
Swabian and
Bavarian Rococo.

Le pèlerinage des
Vierzehnheiligen
(1743–72) joue le
même rôle dans l'art
rococo franconien que
le font Ottobeuren et
«La Wies» en
Souabe et en Bavière.

← Schmidt-Glaßner

Franken, Land des Barock. Oben: Kapitäl in der Wallfahrtskirche Vierzehnheiligen.
Rechts: Blick in das großartige Treppenhaus des bischöflichen Schlosses Pommersfelden, des frühesten großen Barockschlosses in Franken.

130

Schloßverwaltung

Left page: Detail from Baroque Vierzehnheiligen Church. Above: Magnificent staircase of Pommersfelden Castle, a former bishop's palace.
Page gauche: Chapiteau dans l'Eglise des Vierzehnheiligen. Au dessus: L'escalier magnifique de l'ancien palais épiscopal de Pommersfelden.

Luftbild der ehrwürdigen Bischofsstadt Bamberg mit dem alten Rathaus über der Regnitz.

Air view of Bamberg, venerable episcopal seat for many centuries, with the old town hall above the Regnitz.

Vue aérienne de la vénérable ville épiscopale de Bamberg avec le vieil hôtel de ville au-dessus de la Regnitz.

Wolff & Tritschler

Über Bambergs Altstadt hinaus ragt der mächtige doppelchörige Dom der Stauferzeit mit seinen vier Türmen.

The mighty cathedral of Bamberg with its two choirs and four spires towers above the old part of the town.

Au-dessus de la ville vieille de Bamberg s'élance la puissante cathédrale à deux chœurs, de l'époque des Hohenstaufen, et ses quatre tours.

Bambergs Kaiserdom
birgt eine stolze Fülle
klassischer deutscher Plastik,
darunter (links) das Grab-
mal Kaiser Heinrichs II.
von Tilmann Riemen-
schneider und den
„Bamberger Reiter" (um
1235, rechts), das Sinnbild
christlich-abendländischen
Rittertums.

In Bamberg Cathedral,
a wealth of classical
German art treasures can
be seen, among them
Henry II's tomb
(left) and the
"Bamberg Knight" (1235,
right) the highest symbol
of Christian chivalry in
the Middle Ages.

La cathédrale de Bamberg
est riche en trésors d'art
classiques, dont le tombeau
d'Henri II (à gauche), et le
«Chevalier de Bamberg»
(1235, à droite), symbole
le plus élevé de la
chevalerie chrétienne au
Moyen Age.

←— · Hege —→

135

Busch

Nürnbergs Wahrzeichen, der Sinwellturm seiner Burg, ragt noch heute . . .

Nuremberg's landmark, the Sinwell Tower of the castle, still stands proudly . . .

La Tour Sinwell du château, symbole de Nuremberg, existe toujours . . .

Aufsberg

*. . . während das alte Nürnberg zu Füßen der Kaiserburg mit den charakteristischen Silhouetten der Kirchen fast ganz in Trümmer sank.
Was heute neu entsteht, ist eine moderne Stadt mit alten Kunstdenkmälern. (Vorkriegsaufnahme.)*

*. . . whereas old Nuremberg at the foot of the Kaiserburg, with its characteristic silhouettes of churches, was transformed into a heap of rubble.
Today there emerges a modern town with some old artistic monuments.*

*. . . tandis que les flèches du vieux Nuremberg, dessinées fièrement contre le ciel, furent détruites de fond en comble.
Il en surgit aujourd'hui une ville moderne enrichie de quelques monuments d'art.*

137

*Nürnberg. Der prächtige Chor der Lorenzkirche (1439–77) mit dem Englischen Gruß (Verkündigung Mariae, 1517) von Veit Stoss
und dem Sakramentshaus von Adam Kraft (1493).*

Nuremberg. The magnificent choir of St. Laurence's (1439–77) with the Annunciation (Veit Stoss 1517) and Adam Kraft's tabernacle (1493).

Nuremberg. Le chœur magnifique de l'église St. Laurent (1439–77), contenant l'Annonciation (Veit Stoss 1517) et le tabernacle (1493), œuvre d'Adam Kraft.

138

Der Hof des Pellerhauses (1605) als schönstes Beispiel der vielen jetzt zerstörten Patrizierhäuser,
an denen Nürnberg reich war.

The courtyard of the Pellerhaus (1605), the most beautiful of all Nuremberg's numerous mansions now destroyed.

La cour de la Maison Peller, détruite, le plus beau de tous les vieux hôtels de Nuremberg (1605).

Busch

Nürnberg. Das Wohnhaus Albrecht Dürers, vom Kriege hart mitgenommen, steht wieder.
Es ist jetzt Mittelpunkt eines der wenigen inselartig noch erhaltenen altertümlichen Bezirke dieser einstmals so unvergleichlichen Stadt.

The badly damaged house of Albrecht Dürer is now the centre of one of the few islands of undestroyed old buildings still left in Nuremberg.

La maison d'Albrecht Durer, qui a beaucoup souffert des raids aériens, se trouve au milieu d'un des rares îlots de vieux bâtiments à Nuremberg.

Blick aus Dürers Arbeitszimmer zur Burg.

View from Dürer's study onto the castle.

Le château, vu du cabinet de travail d'Albrecht Durer.

Nördlich Nürnberg liegt Erlangen, bekannt als hohe Schule des Geistes.
Das Collegienhaus der Universität.

Well known as a great centre of learning, Erlangen lies to the North of Nuremberg.
Partial view of the university ("Collegienhaus").

Erlangen, au nord de Nuremberg, est bien connu comme grand centre intellectuel.
Vue partielle de l'université (« Collegienhaus »).

Besonders hübsch ist das Tal der Wiesent bei Gößweinstein
in der „Fränkischen Schweiz".

The Wiesent valley
near Gössweinstein in "Franconian Switzerland" is specially beautiful.

Le vallon du Wiesent
près de Gossweinstein en «Suisse Franconienne» est d'une beauté toute spéciale.

Das Nabburger Tor der alten Stadt Amberg in der Oberpfalz.

The Nabburg Gate of the old town of Amberg in the Upper Palatinate.

La Porte de Nabburg de la vieille ville d'Amberg dans le Haut Palatinat.

Metz

144

Der Markt Kallmünz an der Naab liegt am Ostrand des Fränkischen Jura.

The market town of Kallmünz on the river Naab lies at the eastern fringe of the Franconian Jura.

Le bourg de Kallmunz sur Naab se trouve à la lisière Est du Jura Franconien.

Busch

Die wohlerhaltene Ausstattung des Markgrafenschlosses in Ansbach, der Kreishauptstadt Mittelfrankens, sucht ihresgleichen.

The interior decoration and furnishings of the Margraves' castle at Ansbach, now the centre of Central Franconia, have yet to find their parallel.

L'ameublement incomparable du château des Margraves d'Ansbach, aujourd'hui chef-lieu de la Moyenne Franconie.

146

Gundermann

Bayreuth, die Stadt der Richard-Wagner-Festspiele, besitzt in dem Markgräflichen Opernhaus den besterhaltenen Barocktheaterbau Deutschlands.

Bayreuth, famous for its Richard Wagner festival, has in its opera house the best-preserved Baroque theatre in Germany.

Baireuth, renommé pour son Festival Richard Wagner, peut se vanter du théâtre baroque le mieux conservé de l'Allemagne.

Gundermann

Die reich dekorierte Hofseitenfassade der Plassenburg bei Kulmbach (1559–69), ein schönes Beispiel der schmuckfreudigen deutschen Renaissance-Architektur.

Plassenburg near Kulmbach. The ornate rear facade (1559–69) is a fine example of decorative German Renaissance architecture.

Plassenburg près de Kulmbach. La façade nord surchargée d'ornements est un bel exemple de l'architecture décorative allemande de la Renaissance.

Höch-Bavaria

Das Gymnasium Casimirianum ist ein besonders interessantes Baudenkmal in Coburg. Herzog Johann Casimir ließ es 1601 errichten.

The Casimirianum Grammar School, erected by Duke John-Casimir in 1601, is a specially interesting building in Coburg.

Le Lycée Casimirianum, érigé à Coburg par le Duc Jean-Casimir en 1601, est d'un intérêt particulier.

149

Renner

Renner →

Das waldreiche Fichtelgebirge, die Begrenzung Frankens nach Nordosten hin, besteht aus Urgestein. Blick von der Kösseine (938 m) bei Wunsiedel zum Ochsenkopf.

The well-wooded slopes of the Fichtelgebirge, bounding N. E. Franconia, consist of igneous rock. View of the Ochsenkopf, taken from the Kösseine peak near Wunsiedel (3173 ft.).

La Franconie est bornée au N. E. par les montagnes boisées du Fichtelgebirge, composées de roche pyrogène. L'Ochsenkopf, vu du sommet du Kösseine près de Wunsiedel (938 m.).

Der Frankenwald, der sich nach Norden zu an das Fichtelgebirge anschließt, ist mit seinen Burgen und alten Städtchen als Landschaft noch kaum entdeckt. Burg Lauenstein.

The Franconian Forest, the northern fringe of which borders the Fichtel Mountains, is still practically undiscovered. Lauenstein Castle.

La Forêt Franconienne, limitée au nord par les montagnes du Fichtelgebirge, est encore pratiquement inconnue. Le château de Lauenstein.

Aufsberg

*Die eigenartige Wallfahrtskirche Kappl bei Waldsassen wurde 1635 im nördlichen
Zipfel der Oberpfalz errichtet, mit dem Dreipaß als Grundriß.*

*The singular pilgrimage church of Kappl near Waldsassen was built at the northern
tip of the Upper Palatinate in 1635, when this part of the country was annexed to Bavaria.*

*L'église singulière de Kappl, lieu de pèlerinage près de Waldsassen, fut construite
en 1635 à l'extrême nord du Haut Palatinat lors de l'annexion bavaroise.*

Groth-Schmachtenberger

Totenbretter bei Lam, wie sie zwischen Osser und Arber den Wanderer durch den Bayerischen Wald begleiten.
These wooden memorials often meet the eye of travellers through the Bavarian Forest between Osser and Arber.
Ces monuments funéraires en bois frappent souvent les regards des promeneurs s'attardant entre Osser et Arber dans la Forêt Bavaroise.

153

Zwiesel ist der Mittelpunkt der Holz- wie der Glasindustrie des Bayerischen Waldes, der Landschaft eines Adalbert Stifter.

Zwiesel is the centre of the wood and glass industries in the Bavarian Forest.

Zwiesel, centre industriel de la Forêt Bavaroise, renommé pour le bois et la verrerie.

154

Metz

Burgruine Weissenstein bei Regen am gleichnamigen Flüßchen.

The ruined castle of Weissenstein near Regen, a town on the river of the same name.

Le château en ruines de Weissenstein près de Regen, petite ville abreuvée par la rivière du même nom.

Der hübsche Marktplatz von Regen.

Regen Market Place.

La Place du Marché de Regen.

Schmidt-Glaßner

Straubing, jetzt Amtsstadt in der fruchtbaren Donauebene, war lange Zeit die Residenz des Herzogtums Niederbayern.
Fast südländisch — und doch typisch bayerisch ist dieser Innenhof.

Straubing, now an administrative centre in the fertile Danube plain, was for a long time the seat of the Dukes of Lower Bavaria.
This inner courtyard has almost a southern air.

Straubing, aujourd'hui centre administratif situé dans la plaine fertile du Danube, fut pendant longtemps la résidence des Ducs de la Bavière Inférieure.
Cette cour a quelquechose de méridional.

Die Grenzstadt Passau liegt malerisch am Zusammenfluß von Inn (oben), Donau (unten) und Ilz.

The frontier town of Passau lies picturesquely at the confluence of the Inn, Danube, and Ilz.

Passau, ville de frontière, est situé pittoresquement au confluent de l'Inn, du Danube, et de l'Ilz.